35.00

FOOTDREAMS AND TREETALES

ELLIOT R. WOLFSON

Footdreams + Treetales

NINETY-TWO POEMS

FORDHAM UNIVERSITY PRESS  NEW YORK 2007

Copyright © 2007 Fordham University Press

All rights reserved. No part of this publication
may be reproduced, stored in a retrieval system,
or transmitted in any form or by any means—
electronic, mechanical, photocopy, recording,
or any other—except for brief quotations in
printed reviews, without the prior permission
of the publisher.

Library of Congress Cataloging-in-Publication Data

Wolfson, Elliot R.
Footdreams and treetales : 92 poems / Elliot R. Wolfson.—1st ed.
    p.   cm.
ISBN 978-0-8232-2820-1 (alk. paper)
I. Title.
PS3623.O587F66   2007
811.6—dc22

2007025685

Printed in the United States of America
09 08 07   5 4 3 2 1

First edition

to virginia

for helping me
remember what
                we must forget

contents

foreword xi

preface xxiii

NINETY-TWO POEMS

old tale 1

walking pause/erection uprooted 2

winged purple 3

concept less 4

friday's hymn 5

elijah's cup 6

celibacy 7

key of oblivion 8

on the way/at home 10

the warden 11

self-reliance 12

deflecting 13

judgment 14

by guilt innocent 16

predictable ambivalence 17

infinite redress 18

on the cross/entangled and detached 20

do not lay still 23

from before/until
    after   25

deliverance   27

regressing forward   29

double vision   30

cracks & crevices   31

reversal   32

if i found myself
    sought   33

retinal repercussions   34

necrology   35

night's disorder   36

festival of light   38

there was a time   40

seven virgins   41

beyond river   43

moon shoe   44

dark mirror   45

imprint   46

foreskin   47

hourglass   49

drifting   50

from dust   51

breakwater   52

vestige   54

prayertrace   55

timepiece   57

time to let go   59

six thousand nails   61

decollated   62

at sabbath gate   63

through walls   65

be   66

do not pray with
   feet   67

through her veil   68

talitha kumi   69

skydrain   70

hail mary   72

virility/sterile   73

summons   74

with new feet   75

cuttingbone   76

sky earth   77

doubt   78

fish clap   79

abgrund   80

timed zone   81

timefracture   82

ecliptical   83

already broken   84

break bread   85

deathleap   86

teacup moon   87

wheelflight 88

terminus 89

night flight 90

bhagavati 91

mixing waters 92

ice cubed 93

river swerve 94

pigeon jangle 95

fingerprint 96

retrograde 97

schon zeit 98

breathing bones 99

awake 100

dharmadhâtu 101

time rush 102

killing time 103

death-in-time 104

nirodha 105

prey for peace 106

monkey mind 107

kapici bashi 108

vâsanâ 109

a/rose 110

foreword | BARBARA E. GALLI

[Art] . . . must be the axe for the frozen sea inside us.
| —FRANZ KAFKA

Poetry is the great art of constructing transcendental sanity. Therefore the poet is a transcendental physician.
| —NOVALIS

Those who are versed in any of Elliot Wolfson's academic writings will note—as already explicitly noted by many—that his scholarly prose, too, is poetically cast. The poetics are evident in at least a twofold sense: on the one hand, in the poetic diction, tone and style and, on the other, in an espousal of intrinsically poetic modes of logic, in particular that of coincidences of opposites. Wolfson's first major work, *Through a Speculum That Shines: Vision and Imagination in Medieval Jewish Mysticism* (Princeton University Press, 1994), recipient of the National Jewish Book Award and the American Academy of Religion Book Award, while it gives ample evidence of that twofold poetic sense, it does so in a more covert or disguised way than is apparent in his more recent books. Right in the title of one book, for example, we find the word "poetic": *Language, Eros, Being: Kabbalistic Hermeneutics and Poetic Imagination* (Fordham University Press,

2005), another recipient of the National Jewish Book Award. It is evident in most of his publications that, along with his immersion in the scholarly materials, Wolfson is in constant conversation as well with the thought and works of poets —Blake, Celan, Leonard Cohen, Bob Dylan, Dickinson, Hölderlin, and Rilke, to name a few. Often, he places as chapter or article headings several pertinent lines from a poem, and he discusses poets' insights within the body of his texts.

Further, those who have read Wolfson (or, for that matter, have heard him offer a public lecture) also have regularly noted that his precision of intellectual enquiry, his hermeneutical acuity and articulateness, and his boldly creative thinking are soundly based on a breathtakingly vast background of his (ongoing) multidisciplinary research. The content of his poems also demonstrate this firm foundation. Scholars repeatedly remark, and not lightly so, that Wolfson is nothing short of a genius.

Finally, anyone in touch with Wolfson's work would note that his expertise spans, in depth, several disciplines. Among these are included philology; hermeneutics; ancient, medieval and modern philosophy (both Western and Asian); philosophy of religion; comparative religions; as well as that for which he is to date most recognized—Jewish mysticism and comparative mysticisms. Given all this, while it is a supreme honor to present this foreword, it is difficult to write about poems that are so exceedingly rich and multiplex that to say anything is at the same time lamentably to omit much else that ought to be said, or, worse, regrettably to interrupt what others might see better if the poems are surrounded by silence. What Titus Burckhardt once wrote with regard to the transconscious role of tradition in sacred architecture and artworks serves as a fitting description of what is behind and in Wolfson's poetry. He states that "tradition . . . guarantees the spiritual validity of the forms. Tradition has within itself a secret force." This force, moreover, is, in Burckhardt's words, one "that neither the artists themselves nor the subsequent users entirely understand." The situation with Wolfson's poems is in addition complicated and enriched by the fact that his poems are not merely shaped by more than one tradition but also actively participate in the growth and reshaping of various religions, whether individually or in their interactions.

The poems are not so much an offshoot of Wolfson's academic work, but are interconnected with it. His poems, very often, are saying that which, at a particular moment, he is involved with in his scholarship, and it is safe to say that one of the contributions of this collection would be the application of the view that (contra Plato) there is a convergence between philosophy and poetry. An obvious example from *Footdreams and Treetales* is found in lines from the poem "seven virgins": "facing the effaced / in love's mirror." And, in 1997 an article by Wolfson appeared that is entitled "Facing the Effaced: Mystical Eschatology and the Idealistic Orientation in the Thought of Franz Rosenzweig." Readers of the poems may find many more examples; indeed, all the poems are steeped in philosophical and theological traditions. It is, of course, telling that the collection here begins with the poem "old tale," a reflection on creation.

A few words, anecdotally presented, about various receptions of Wolfson's poems may prove helpful. Several years ago, on two separate occasions, I shared with two prominent academics a few of Wolfson's unpublished poems that he had given to me (and he will give poems to anyone who expresses an interest). Lawrence Kaplan, a McGill professor of medieval Jewish studies, actually to my surprise, showed great enthusiasm and understanding, having picked up at once on the biblical and mystical motifs and references, and having been taken with the tone, rhythm, and originality. Zayn Kassam, a scholar of Islamic studies, told me at a conference, with a kind of awe, that she saw it as partly my responsibility to convince Wolfson to start publishing collections of his poems. And indeed, the first collection of sixty poems was published in the volume *Pathwings: Philosophic and Poetic Reflections on the Hermeneutics of Time and Language* (Station Hill Press, 2004). Until that time, over the years, only single poems had appeared in print, for instance in the learned magazine *Tikkun*. *Pathwings*, as a whole, with its overarching theme of time, can be read as a companion to one of Wolfson's recent books: *Alef, Mem, Tau: Kabbalistic Musings on Time, Truth, and Death* (University of California Press, 2006). The press that published *Pathwings*, however, unfortunately insisted on framing that collection with several of Wolfson's articles that had been previously published, a plan that Wolfson resisted in vain. For *Footdreams and Treetales*, my hope is that, though this foreword is already too much peripheral material, it does not detract from simply reading the poems, one by one, slowly and repeatedly, and never turning back again to these pages of the foreword.

In the meantime, to continue with the anecdotes, at a chapel service at McGill, I had occasion to read aloud two of Wolfson's poems. Afterward, the well-known Catholic theologian Gregory Baum approached me, saying that usually he considers himself to be lacking in a poetic sensibility but that these poems he found forcible, brilliant, and very moving. In Baum's case, I suspect the attraction is in part due to Wolfson's brand of reverence. Like Baum's, Wolfson's theological struggles push the limits close to what at first sight might seem to border on irreverence. There is a combination in the poems of linguistic elegance and (if I may put it this way) bluntness. Yet the complaints, the laments, the pain, are all eloquent expressions reminiscent of the Psalmist's in the face of distortions on earth of divine truth that come in the shape of deceit and other such human shortcomings. The reverent "irreverence," too, bespeaks a kind of hope by the very fact that the poems read as if addressing someone. A sense of hope and even comfort, as sharp and painful as most of the poems are, is therefore felt in the poetically implied facts that there *are* things to lament, that there *is* "someone" to whom to address the laments, that what seems inexpressible *can* be expressed, and that there *is* something to aspire to.

In several classes at McGill between 2001 and 2004, and before that at the University of Alabama between 1997 and 1999, I had the opportunity to teach portions of several courses using Wolfson's poetry. The courses were in the field of philosophy of religion: Religion and the Arts, at the 300 level; and The Thought of Franz Rosenzweig, at the 400 level. Admittedly, each time, I worried about reception among undergraduates, and I introduced and assigned the poems with reservations and trepidation. Yet the students—from such diverse disciplines as from religious studies to finance, from political science and law to psychology—each found the poems keenly "speaking" to them and appealingly challenging. Each wrote remarkably insightful analyses and responses; and both the students and I found the class discussions engaging, valuable, and fascinating. Clearly, there is a lot more to see in the poems than what I have so far seen. One of the poems I introduced was especially welcomed and favored: "breakwater." To this day, former students speak of the transformative effects that the poems have had on them. They say that what they most remember about those classes was Wolfson's poetry, and the day he visited the class.

The matter with the students is not as facile as I may be making it sound here. Reflective in Wolfson's poetry there is a logic, mentioned above, or a mindset that he has mastered (along with the great poets, like Blake), which Wolfson deems to be prevalent too in the kabbalistic worldview: a logic of coincidence of opposites. Wolfson, however, through the hermeneutics of his kabbalistic studies, has taken this notion, philosophically and theologically, a step further. He spells out coincidences of opposites as opposites that are opposite *because they are the same*. This notion, ungraspable by linear logic, and only fleetingly graspable by a logic of opposites, arises out of a seeking to understand the profundity of the thinking through what monotheism means. Subsequent to and concurrent with his studies in kabbalah and other mystical and philosophical modalities, Wolfson determined that this logic of opposites resonates strikingly in certain thinkers, notably (besides in poets) in Heidegger, to whose thought Wolfson has given much attention. The more (and the more often) one reads Wolfson's poems, the notion of opposites as he sees it becomes clearer. Indeed the students reported that thinking this way made clearer for them more familiar forms of logic; and that the logic of opposites helped them to make better practical sense of the world. To work through this unusual way of thinking, to convey it to others in such a way as not to arrive at levels of the absurd or nihilism, is, in my view, one of the contributions of Wolfson's poems. It is at that apparently (and real) clashing of opposites, points of differentiation, that knowledge of all sorts, intellectual and emotional at once, can best be enhanced. The title alone, for instance, of "by guilt innocent," a poem also read with the students, shows one of the ways in which Wolfson evokes coincidences of opposites. It is one thing to say this discursively, it is another to express it and to show it in poems. According to Wolfson, poetry and philosophy converge and can reflect one another, but they are far from identical or interchangeable modes of speaking. That poems speak to the mind as well as to the heart is reflected in the title of another collection of Wolfson's poems: *Secrets of the Heartland: 32 Poems* (2004).

The name that Wolfson has given to his entire collection, a collection that continually grows, is "preparations for death." This notion may also be a reason for the appeal that I have noted by so many: The poems read like prayers. There is a courageous and lucid opening of the soul. This very baring of the soul, however, also played a part in my reservations at using poems in a classroom setting. I worried: Would the students be unduly disturbed by the expressions of pain? But, like me, they found them uncannily soothing. It seems that the precision of language, the unflinching facing of pain, and the poetizing of pain into linguistic beauty without anaesthetization, all together perform another sort of coincidence of opposites: the placing of pain and beauty alongside each other such that neither overwhelms nor denies the other. Perhaps it is the undeniability of the beauty on the one hand and the pain on the other that is soothing. What soothes readers more so may be the thought and the ideas that are housed in the poems. That is to say, the difficult, simultaneously unsettling *thinking* that is stimulated through the poems on the reader's part is what turns out to be soothing. Maybe it is the affirmation that such seemingly inexpressible thoughts and feelings can be thought and expressed. The emotion, the feeling, in every single poem will be seen to be tied seamlessly as one with heart, mind, soul, and body.

If one were simply to read the table of contents, one would see that the list of titles alone reads as if it were a poem. Or, if one were merely to flip though the pages of this book, it would be enough to gauge the varieties of length, shape, mood, and styles entailed here, which is evidence of the care with which Wolfson organized and arranged this collection.

Some poems rhyme, some do not. Some poems comprise lines that are made up only of single words (see, for example, "judgment," "deliverance," "if i found myself sought," "hourglass," "through walls," and "hail mary"). Grammatically, the poems of single-word lines read in a multitude of interesting ways, deliberately ambiguous—or showing instances of a logic of both-and, rather than either-or. Other poems are weightier in the length of their lines, and some of these read like stories. A few show exact or inexact mirror images between several lines at beginnings and endings of poems (see, for instance, "cracks & crevices," "at sabbath gate," "ecliptical"). These mirror images are much less literary devices than they are depictions of a philosophy of reading (and relating), as delineated in

Through a Speculum That Shines and in "seven virgins" (mentioned earlier). And all this counts, line lengths, and numbers of lines, and explicit mention of numbers—quite literally counts, for numerology or gematria, too, is a feature of the poetry. Poems connected with Zen Buddhism include "imprint," "dharmadhâtu," and "monkey mind."

Some poems have shockingly harsh phrasings, such as in "prayertrace": "hollow be your name." (This, incidentally, was one of the poems I read in the chapel and that appealed to Gregory Baum.) Or, the short poem "breathing bones": "still / breathing / bones / abiding / disjointedly." Or, in "do not pray with feet," we have lines that read: "do not pray with feet / nor dream with teeth . . . wave cleft / weave claw / swelling feet / wings gnaw / rat throat / roach lip." The poem "schon zeit" includes the very painful lines: "thunder wrench / suicide stench / sea-foam sandstone / sunburned skeleton . . . time walk naked / in shroud of time."

Still other poems are composed for liturgical occasions, like the Jewish New Year; or in memory of someone, as the poem "deathleap," written explicitly in memory of the philosopher Gillian Rose.

Examples of poems that offer a kind of soft, gentle, yearning and especially prayerful mood include "concept less" (a clear reference to philosophical thinking, with allusions to kabbalistic imagination—notably trees—and that begins: "all enveloped / pooling beyond / fringe of intellect /

touching trees"); "be" (which opens with the lines: "there is a dream / that dreams itself / before the dream begins"); and "with new feet," strikingly encouraging in tone and metaphors. Several poems have lines that read like wisdom sayings: "love shall / conquer all / but love / of conquest" (in "deflecting"); and: "love is not / the stuff / of which / love is made" (in "vâsanâ").

There are so many motifs and themes that it would not be feasible to discuss them all here, but this much warrants mentioning: the notion of the path and the (related) questions of birth and death. The final poem, among many throughout this collection, is explicit in the latter theme. This notion of the path is consonant with the rhythm of walking, with the beats of song. Especially suited to song are: "friday's hymn," "predictable ambivalence," "do not lay still," "foreskin." They evoke, too, the songs of Bob Dylan and Leonard Cohen, two important influences on Wolfson. The significance of the idea of being on a path is shown in the title of Wolfson's collection of essays, *Along the Path: Studies in Kabbalistic Myth, Symbolism, and Hermeneutics* (SUNY Press, 1995) and is mirrored in the poem "on the way / at home." Here, for Wolfson, to be on the way is to be at home, a reflection discussed in Jeffrey J. Kripal's chapter "The Mystical Mirror of Hermeneutics: Gazing into Elliot Wolfson's *Speculum* (1995)" (in *Roads of Excess, Palaces of Wisdom: Eroticism and Reflexivity in the Study of Mysticism*, University of Chicago Press, 2001).

Thus, besides the worth of just reading the poems, there is much worth as well in studying them, or rereading them regularly, so complex is each. Each poem could profitably be parsed, and the parsing could turn into an article or essay. Part of the contribution of this work, then, involves a leading to, or a deeper engagement with or understanding of, Wolfson's significance as a thinker, whether gleaned in his poetry or in his prose or in both.

I'll conclude by mentioning two factors in the timeliness for publishing *Footdreams and Treetales*. In the spring of 2007, I had a book come out called *On Wings of Moonlight: Elliot R. Wolfson's Poetry in the Path of Rosenzweig and Celan* (McGill-Queen's University Press, 2007). (The main title is a line in one of Wolfson's poems.) The two (fully positive) readers' reports for this manuscript stressed the importance of Wolfson's poems in connection with his scholarly writings as well as the compelling beauty of his poetry. Now, with Wolfson's recent award for *Language, Eros, Being*, which was handsomely published by Fordham University Press, the collection of poems will very most likely enjoy a large readership from diverse intellectual communities. Whereas Wolfson's scholarly writings and his poems may be mutually elucidating, both of these modes of expression shine with their own light. The difference with the poetic mode is the immediacy of reflection, from the soul of the poet to the soul of a reader, where silence and light stream around the dazzling holiness of the poeticization of truths.

preface

The ninety-two poems included in *Footdreams and Treetales* were chosen from hundreds of poetic offerings that span several decades. The poems reflect the interests that have shaped my scholarly prose—to wit, the study of philosophy, the history of religions, and particularly the mystical dimensions of Judaism, Christianity, Islam, Hinduism, Taoism, and Buddhism. I view the poems as paintings in which I attempt to render visible the invisible. Although explicit references to the divine are rarely found in the poems, I consider them as issuing from my encounter with the mystery of transcendence whose inaccessibility is only enhanced by any effort to access it. The poems, consequently, are mystical in nature, as they embody a hermeneutic of esotericism, the duplicity of the secret, the dialectic of concealment and disclosure, which is predicated on the paradox that what is disclosed can be disclosed only to the extent that it is concealed, but it can be concealed only to the extent that it is disclosed. Although it is difficult to reduce the poems to a simple description, I would say that on the whole they attempt to articulate, in the words of Baudelaire, the inner voice of the ''language of the flowers and other unspeakable things.'' From this voice issues forth a verbal response that is the unsaying that makes possible all saying, even the saying of the impossible—a saying possible precisely because impossible—a response always on the way, a word yet spoken, the thought that cannot be thought, not even in being unthought; this response may be imagined in liturgical terms as the entreaty not captured in words of conventional prayer, but in the contemplative gaze of what eludes contemplation—the present that comes to be in the future awaiting its past. The poem is an opening to time, which is, at once, an embrace of life and a preparation for death.

FOOTDREAMS AND TREETALES

old tale

on moonless eve
she pushed he
into Tree
of Recognition;
he lost her mind
but found his heart

walking pause/erection uprooted

walking pause

erased sunset

reticent nature

this dusk

momentary

vanishing

eternal spark

frightless fall

foot finality

death dangle

beyond distance

measurable

winged purple

winged purple

starlite dust

ending day

night must

concept less

all enveloped

pooling beyond

fringe of intellect

touching trees

watching winds

sensing seas

we be these

and more besides

and more besides

friday's hymn

pour oil on my head,

before the burning ends,

let us rise to count the minutes,

to dot the hours,

let us rise to wake the children

who must bury the dead.

night approaches day,

neither black nor white,

her sun is my moon.

elijah's cup

enter clock

dating pulse

limit time

negating bound

fiery bush

glowing down

endless speech

without sound

through other

in enter

desire pain

remember

...easts

and vacant space

where i become

more consumed

not knowing

crown has fallen

from ground

like crumbs

she bakes

to feed

her name

to the nameless

she delivered

in glut of hunger

he believed love to be

key of oblivion

before birth

of father

death of son

redemptively forlorn

like isaac unbound

in binding sound

to vision entwined

in space spun round

torment in time

tossed by fling

bindingly flung

tarnishing stones

she swallowed

from words

hollow and heavy

repeatedly new

newly repeated

silence spoken

poem between poem

wistfully woven

from transgression

tattered and torn

seam of soul

joyously weeping

at deception

i had become

candidly

frivolous god

worshipped pain

famished flesh

fervent faith

weary and wet

written not yet

on the way / at home

a thousand births

have i died

this life

to rise

in fallenness

of time

thrown back

in forward push

returning beyond

nothing more to seek

but seeking that ends

a thousand deaths

before this birth

in coming-to-be

of what i am not

the warden

angel of death lead me into chamber of peace
where poet washes stain of blood from face of moon,
and the bride watches the prostitute behind the gate
hiding the soles of her feet in the shoes of remorse,
forsaken in the hope born when optimism dies
on the floor of the door that opens without and closes within
the mumbo-jumbo of the wisest sophistry,
illogicality, irrationality, casuistry,
perverting the mind by the cadence of her blow
bellowing beneath unclouded surface of despair,
obtuse the optic angle obfuscated
by flood of moonlight faint and purple perfume
smattered on wall of love like silence of tomb
where the crusted past, discarded and embalmed,
mortifies the morning with impurity of heart
bleeding from nail driven through eye of storm,
in chamber of peace only the prisoner is free,
discharging the warden from restraint of his liberty.

self-reliance

the void

of itself

fully void

beckons

space curve

looping round

time fold

for us perhaps

nothing left

to grasp

if only

we had hands

bound by

open faith

to believe the fiction

that fiction is no fiction

but only a tale flesh tells

in the burning of its flame,

frozen beneath the grave

of love's resurrection

deflecting

deflecting

fractures

formlessly

inflecting

infected

wound

fettered

shroud

shredded

sanguinity—

love shall

conquer all

but love

of conquest

judgment

menstruating
priest
resuscitate
peace
stained
moon
sanctioned
wither
sparrow
climb
verbal
slither
hiding
soul
flayed
horse
forsaken
harp
timbered
voice
opening
without
opening
within
hollow
cadence
bending
tooth

smatter
fragrance
scenting
silence
crusted
words
discarded

by guilt innocent

by guilt innocent

proclaimed judge

suspending bridge

wholeheartedly fragmented

like sugar in tea

dissolved to be

to sweeten other

composedly deconstructed

predictable ambivalence

in synagogue of satan rise pillar of lust
ascending like rime from burning of lamb,
then fell fires of fate upon corpse of time,
waiting to walk on path in forest rhyme,
where poetic rage is holy and saintly sin profound
to all but spirits blinded by visions unseen in sight,
passion the key that opens secret never told
in furnace of faith trembling from raging cold,
prophets groan at specter of incandescent flesh
sealed in book opened through closure of text,
dismal the bliss in suffering of fractured whole
where love eternal dissolved into ephemeral gold,
but to trespass law one must be lawfully bound
to wisdom throne uncovered beneath folly uprooted
lies future folded like scroll of inscripted erasure
by winds that wail in constant pain of sudden pleasure.

infinite redress

entangled the time
in hope of relief,
twisted the space
by rope of belief,
no things remain
that cannot be seen
in mirror broken
by dreams of sin,
washing bones
with scent of death
in the breathless breath
of beast that lay
between night and day,
waiting to sing
morning song
at tomb
where poets burn
and lovers freeze,
beneath the word
reasonably absurd
that lovers speak
in darkness weak
from lust that leak
its greenish blood
on golden pond
glistening in guilt
gilded in debt,

laid in back
like sword of sorrow,
come today
thrust tomorrow

on the cross / entangled and detached

to chain the pull
that pulls the chain
on northbound train
where darkness bleed
from incision of light
ripped open
by stitch of faith
weaving doubt
lingering about
other side of moon
beyond the pride
where truth lied
time and again
after he knew
her steps misled
on track that bled
him to death
in guise of life
mistress misery
mystery set free
nothingness that be
divulging sin
buried within
guarded not
dying begun
being undone
river waiting
to be wet

dream
concretely lean
waxing flesh
curse to bless
misgiving taken
this way that way
ding dong
dong ding
mother proffer
what child bring
broken ring
in difference
to pull the chain
that chains the pull
on southbound train
where light proliferate
condensation of dark
into timeless spark
threaded by time
become space
divine waste
disgrace
dong the ding
ding the dong
short long
middle margin
all white cows black
all black cows white
in depth
shimmering beneath
wham of whim
holiness sin

holding in letting go
vision sublime
nothing is everything
that nothing be

do not lay still

do not
lay still
on the spot
where love lingers
untied in knot
of resignation
filled with privation,
and time chases
tail of serpent
untold by tongue
that longs to repent—
god, god, god
hiss . . .
the serpent snarl
before deaf ears
the judge stands trial

peace to father
laid to sleep
on dreams of death
content in regret,
peace to mother
aroused to wake
by charge of faith
laden by mirth
that blind the eye
in attempt to fly
above the cloud

of anger and doubt,
blocking the view
of faces that mask
the faces that hide
the shameful pride
of deceit that is true

from before / until after

you and i
eyeing one another
in expanded mirror—
"the bliss be
beside the point,"
said he,
"yet the point
it remains to be,"
said she.
eye alone
cannot see
truth of truth
glare of moon
frozen lake
raging dread
darkened noon
digestible host
laid before
altar of time
smashed
at foot of drum
beating to
silence pounding
idol of self
into image of other
over bridge
under way
to home

once
i and you
brought me back
to where i
was not
before

deliverance

blind
folded
sighting
sight
pondering
plight
panic
swoon
mirror
darkness
mirror
moon
illumine
distance
mindful
oblivion
plodding
premise
lacking
conclusion
folded
blind—
duplicity

truth
mimic
truth's
mimicry

regressing forward

regressing forward

to leap behind

edge of time

reversing toward

margin of dream

unwrit by scum

oozing from scar

opening the seal

of lust licking

wound of word

violently spoken

in voiceless speech

unspeakable

double vision

seemingly,

nothing is what

it seems to be,

but to be it seems,

in the speculum

of her text,

tattered

by exchange

of goods,

so it seems

to be

in the grayness

of dawn,

yearning

to expand

the constriction

upon

the foundation

laid

in the fluidity

of time

before

cracks & crevices

from the first
nothing
was the nothing
that nothing is
lingering like lust
in open crack
cracked open
by foot asunder
in blunder of desire
all beings come
in coming-to-be
of nothing
that was nothing
that nothing is
from the first

reversal

awaiting us the past

not yet become

what has been

vibrating stagnantly

on circumference of chance

fated in destiny free

of domestic demand

and barbaric delusion

what love must be

no longer become the past

not yet become

in this waiting

for what has not been

if i found myself sought

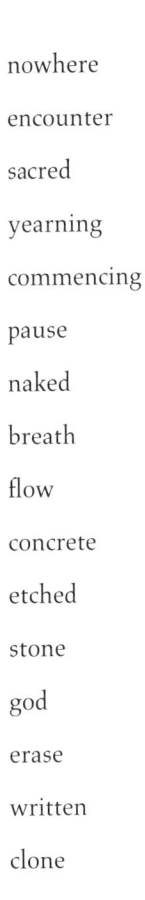

nowhere

encounter

sacred

yearning

commencing

pause

naked

breath

flow

concrete

etched

stone

god

erase

written

clone

retinal repercussions

in shelter exposure

the shadow encircle

thread unraveled

by desire and guilt

imprinted on flesh

flashing like fish

fried in crystal dish

of porcelain passion

crashing against

civility's concern

that scornfully burn

the core to the core

of careless caution

tossed to the wind

where the faithful doubt

it shall end

if it might begin

necrology

crypto-imagination

between birth death

love's graven image

worship nonappearance

replicated difference

desecrated deference

incongruity disjointed

prescriptive-dissimulation

night's disorder

night's

disorder

stacked

against

coiled

shaft

shedding

skin

bolting

mind

to come again

twice as hard

in her yard

where apples lay

in dark cliché

and children pray

to play

beside

dried-out

dream

bare

pearl

whirl

tooth

tongue

tweeting

time

twaddle

festival of light

in darkness
truth glow
behind
the shadow
of thirst
cast
like stone
on sea
of bliss,
before
the light
but after
the darkness
belong
ray of hope
glistening
within
cloud
of doubt,
we rise
to weep
and weep
to rise,
above
the pain,
beyond
the pleasure
where love

is lost
to be found,
excess
of joy
limited
by woe,
overflow
despair
the moment
repair,
a skeleton
this time
in garment
of grief,
tormented
by truth
that mutter
deceit,
holy
the fury
of the
fiery chill,
the flame
that kindle
passion's fluidity

there was a time

there was a time

we washed the eye

to enter key

in memory lock

stock fragment

where poem

used to be

and vision

(trans)muted

become

second key

entering lock

love-struck

night fall

burning bright

seven virgins

seven virgins
within
spin
on pin
punctuating
her point
as he tarries
at door
opened
before
he arrived
but closed
now
that he entered
his tongue
longing
to leak
on parchment
of her secret
to speak
of her trust
hidden beneath
veiled truth
lifted
morning after
beginning's end
within
spin

of four faces
facing the effaced
in love's mirror
darkened and disfigured
the image that is real

beyond river

beyond
river
move
shadow
of light
and
time burn
black tea
in jaded cup
weeping
flesh
flushed
fresh
from
beneath
flashes
night
beyond
doubt
move
shadow
to light
dimly lit
truth slit
love's veil
intact

moon shoe

moon

shoe

eye

print

treading

monoscopically

at window

beckon

awaken

exalted

fear

far

from

forgetfulness

forgotten

this night

love ring

undone

dark mirror

dark
mirror
polish
night
retrieve
lisp
lapse
what
fortune
sarah
cast
in lips
that bite
bitten lips
bleeding dog
ishmael
at hagar's feet
flaxen wheat
coagulate sperm
exploding worm
woken affliction
i am not am i
balaam's face
jacob's ass

imprint

if master
true
be he
let him
dispose
mask
of mastery
and ten
thousand
things
may he see
in darkness deep
blue as night
bleeding light
from love cut
left to swell
beneath
glacial breath
she bore not
in birth of death
we became
more of less

in

the sea
burning
the sea
repeatedly
smashed
on rocks
swirling
in pain
too pleasurable
to heal
love's
battlefield
visibly invisible
for same other
she would become

logic has
no reason
guilt has
no shame
but together
they gather
dust and light
lurching
to hold sway
on broken spoke
threadbare
windblown

the flame
freezing
the flame
fanning
floods of famine
that clasp
heartstring
to spearhead
pointedly blunt
punctuating puncture
already sealed
by foreskin forsaken

hourglass

hour
glass
grind
time
pierce
peace
return
jerusalem
dream
half-dead
dustbin
tailspin
stonethrow
wheelturn
bloodbath
aftermath
distillation
resuscitation

drifting

drifting
cloud
brushing
grain
craving
space
carving
stone
gripping
time
tactless
flow
the law
fastening
fornicating
dreams
in streams
that cut
and mend
mangled hand
open pipe
frozen free
beyond sky
ocean weep

from dust

from
dust
dust,
must
lust
always
be,
never
free

river
wind
mend

all that is
but desire

want
nothing

to remain
nothing

breakwater

more
than
nothing
is nothing
more
than
nothing
that
nothing is

not that this
nor this that

resolutely
midway
betwixt
who & what

circumference-center
balance-point
disjuncture
here-now
s/he

less
than
nothing
is nothing

less
than
nothing
that
nothing is

exposed
through veil
fore/seen
re/collected
footcloud
waterbreaking
stareye
ejaculating
in mouth of mule
on head of bull
wordcut,
firstborn,
tip of tongue
silence sliver

longing,
we belong

1 september 2001
berkeley, california

vestige

smoldering
steel
crumble
creed
rhetorically
defiant

allah loves
his daughters
even those
he slaughters

but sons,
that's another
matter

13 september 2001
new york city

prayertrace

to walk
without trace

to speak
without voice

to hold
without grasp

to be done
in the undone

to be seen
in the unseen

to be born
in the unborn

this,
my will,
fulfill
o mother,
hollow be your name,
overflowing

knowing
the unknowing

my lips leap

to empty
emptiness

to break
brokenness

to hope
hopelessness

rosh ha-shanah 2001
new york city

timepiece

in
name
of
one
who
has
no
name

isaac
bow
breaching
vow
before
altar
thrown
faltering
uncovered
beneath
stone
memory
bone
down
trodden
ground
broken

death is
the flower

looming
from tower
truth dissemble

yom kippur, 2001
new york city

time to let go

"time
to let go,"
he say,
coming
through
the wind
never been
sacred
majestic
whimsical
free
me
she
he
you

mâyâ

"time
to let go,"
she say,
going
out
before
the moon
glowing
dark
reeking

oblivious
alone
own
seed
thrown

samsâra

"time
to let go,"
it say,
standing
firm
moving
death
breathe
clean
semen
flown
down
demand
every
nothing
extinction be

six thousand nails

six

thousand

nails

bind

mind

mist

ignite

violent

trembling

immobile

resolute

moon-lit

sundown

broken

open

love ended

decollated

askew
love lay
yoked free

the eye—
delicate
decollate
accolade
cocked
awry

at sabbath gate

at
sabbath
gate

wait,
love

parting
way

folding
fold

stitching
time

bending
mind

forgive me,
father,
i am no son
this dawn

mind
bending

time
stitching

fold
folding

way
parting

love,
wait

at
sabbath
gate

through walls

through
walls
wallow
ghosts
behind
memory
cracks
crestfallen
jawbreak
heartcleft
jewbleak
time head
silver cup
chewing
spoon
spinning
spleen
spawning
swoon
petitioning
wheel
ascending
down

berlin
11 february 2002

be

there is a dream

that dreams itself

before the dream begins—

a dream dreamt

in the dreamless dream

of a dream

that no longer dreams

except in a dream

do not pray with feet

do not pray
with feet
nor dream
with teeth
encrusted beneath
flesh bequeathed
circumcised tick
withholding prick
puncture time
wave cleft
weave claw
swelling feet
wings gnaw
rat throat
roach lip
sliptongue
end to end
endless end
not be end
ended is

4 july 2002
new york city

through her veil

through

her veil

his voice

i heard

vacated

in time

behind

their nakedness

etched in

stone

the name

we cannot

re/member

to forget

what it was

we remembered

to forget

talitha kumi

rise

this

dawn

down

snow

sown

slope

slush

crush

cellular

brain

crinkling

foam

fed

pheasant

feet

steadily

erode

logic

knocked

astray—

all be none,

if none be all

skydrain

sky

drain

stellar

flow

porcelain

pipe

streaming

up

water

mouth

sprouting

truth

being

time

strapped

time

being

stringing

atoms

dissected

whole

woman

man

imbalance
bland
bind
gender
blind

hail mary

in

mystery,

mystery

hang

bewildered

beads

mirror

glass

beauty

in

mystery,

mystery

hung

virility/sterile

to turn other cheek
with chains & fractured lens
baking bread in nuptial chamber
jerusalem suck solomon's yeast
buried in shepherd's breast
hiding head on mountain tread
soulless feet dew drip seedless
breadcrumbs bare left by desire
water-stained & consummated
in flames of text inscribed on heart
lovers part beneath bow & cloud

summons

combustion

freezing

flowing

flame

kindling

nightlight

daydark

no more

than more

nothing

gain

again

against

all odds

even the even

seem odd

this birth

i cannot breathe

or leave to die

berlin
31 january 2003

with new feet

with new feet

wings shall come

skyward & seabound

breathing stars of sand

in swirl of time

trickling tenuously

on landscape mind

thinking thought unthinkable—

nothing be nothing it be not,

if not for nothing it not be

cuttingbone

embedded

breathlapse

beingmiddle

sky earth

sky earth

earth sky

bridge-whist

time wisp

doubt

dangling
doubt
disjointedly

mimicking
truth
intemperately

assembling
faith
fortuitously

diminishing
love
excessively

fish clap

fish clap

cloud trap

whip lash

shadow flash

being come

coming be

abgrund

on

way

without

wings

or feet

beyond limit

limit limit

time's sign

resigned

timed zone

disk

brisk

disable

bubble

breaking

brook

blindly

confined

coagulated

asunder

left to wander

desolate but fertile

to disperse seed

and gather weed

in hope hung

all but despair

timefracture

blubber

bellow

mumble

forespoken

fracture

time repair

overshadow

ecliptical

before

the mirror

behind

the veil

the veil

behind

the mirror

before

the veil

already broken

aloof

the alef

inflamed

in chain

of shame

freeing guilt

love tilt

lesion askew

break bread

who shall

break bread

baked before

altar wobble

crippled calf

golden eel

bandaged cat

broken seal

deathleap

mourning

sobriety

by noon

intoxicated

lilies

bloom

impassively

burning

cloudburst

bridging

unbridgeable

distance

dismember

vision

in memory
of gillian rose,
somewhere
between san francisco
and the grand canyon,
3 march 2003

teacup moon

look for moon

in teacup light

alight with

love's longing

lips dripping

dew letting go

stone by stone

her garden rose

his dagger thrown

his bloody nose

her scented throne

wheelflight

wheel flight

flickering night

faintly bright

lifted down

faith ensouling

nuptial doubt

breaking bolt

conjugally gaunt

wanting to want

ten thousand paths

returning there

terminus

let us
ease
the way,
weeping,
highspeed
meltdown,
fullblown
american
breakfast—
nothing left
greedy & taunt
stoutly gaunt,
consume omnipresent
absence of naught
but absence that cannot be
absence it must be
in absence of not being
absence it cannot be,
or is it, not be

grand hotel
poughkeepsie
9 may 2003

night flight

o joy on wing of night

comest & goest like wind

thou touch edge of heart

as thread through eye of pin

thirst made thirsty

by salt of ocean spin

though ceaseless in motion

its movement always been

bhagavati

oozing
blood
from
breast
budding
coconut
tree
menstruating
bathing
cat heat
cooling
womb
expanding
contraction
ripening
green
jaded
black
blood
oozing
from
breast
budding
coconut
tree

mixing waters

merging dream

seam to scene

seem obscene

leaning beam

haltingly lean

in seawater

pipedream burn

ice cubed

ice cubed

flammable flesh

nakedly draped

freely enmeshed

swollen thin

swallowed in

love between

stigma & stain

still between

sleep & dream

hope anticipate

impetuous scheme

river swerve

river swerve

brain slain

hung laid

lamp shade

darken bright

pitch-black

mourning night

pigeon jangle

pigeon chatter

jangle chain

clang clink

clutter chink

slink stem

brain burn

(worm)ice

rice-root rigid

grid cascade

remembered (b)ridge

fingerprint

leafing

tooth

mouthing

proof

soothing

sloth

frothing

moth

moving

truth

fully

empty

time flee

what's meant

not to be

resolutely

retrograde

dust on lip

dipped in dew

sifting through

ether's net

digging deep

in pig pen

sin rise

going down

schon zeit

week edge

etched weak

at brink of blink

lightning flinch

thunder wrench

suicide stench

sea-foam sandstone

sunburned skeleton

balloon expunge

emaciated scum

to deathbed clung

time walk naked

in shroud of time

rosh ha-shanah,
27 september 2003
berlin-new york

breathing bones

still

breathing

bones

abiding

disjointedly

awake

brittle whine
visibly blind
loosely bind
bulging wind
squarely round
rimming sound
wafting time
rhyming rhyme

dharmadhâtu

flaxen
skin
serpent
craw
swallow
fire
rain
cloud
charcoal
bright

nothought
unthought
thought not

time rush

time rush
like fire
o'er rock

time pick
ice sealed
love lock

time burn
birthing worm
barely awoke

killing time

sheltering
enfleshed
open sprout
to doubt
duty-bound
limits infringe
stroke of pen
in nick of spot
what is writ not
by hands unwrought
killing time like bees
buzzing silently
round honey dish
fingered prick pain
lick lips pining
what not is writ
abjectly complicit

death-in-time

to

die

on

time

must

time

time

time's

time

to

die

nirodha

seedless

confession

sprouting

disclaimer

cracking

fracture

intact

time sow

less seed

than time

can grow

prey for peace

memory slice

buttered zest

jammed in breast

brimming waxmilk

on drooling christ

thirsting death

that doth not die

monkey mind

woodworm

gashing

stonedream

enshrouded

dreamstone

mashing

wormwood

kapici bashi

pathless
foot
in motion
still
reason
garnering
refuse
on foot
footless
path
still
in motion

vâsanâ

to step

on stone

memory

cast

love is not

the stuff

of which

love is made

4 july 2004
new york city

a/rose

how doth
the rose glisten
in darkness gloom

sifting through
shattered words
in carnage bloom

together apart
nothing-i-am-not
in freedom doom

love exterminate
death of birth
in rousing womb